Who Killed the Sausage King?

A MURDER MYSTERY FARCE

by Roger Karshner

A SAMUEL FRENCH ACTING EDITION

FOUNDED 1830
NEW YORK HOLLYWOOD LONDON TORONTO

SAMUELFRENCH.COM

Copyright © 2009 by Roger Karshner

ALL RIGHTS RESERVED

CAUTION: Professionals and amateurs are hereby warned that *WHO KILLED THE SAUSAGE KING?* is subject to a royalty. It is fully protected under the copyright laws of the United States of America, the British Commonwealth, including Canada, and all other countries of the Copyright Union. All rights, including professional, amateur, motion picture, recitation, lecturing, public reading, radio broadcasting, television and the rights of translation into foreign languages are strictly reserved. In its present form the play is dedicated to the reading public only.

The amateur live stage performance rights to *WHO KILLED THE SAUSAGE KING?* are controlled exclusively by Samuel French, Inc., and royalty arrangements and licenses must be secured well in advance of presentation. PLEASE NOTE that amateur royalty fees are set upon application in accordance with your producing circumstances. When applying for a royalty quotation and license please give us the number of performances intended, dates of production, your seating capacity and admission fee. Royalties are payable one week before the opening performance of the play to Samuel French, Inc., at 45 W. 25th Street, New York, NY 10010.

Royalty of the required amount must be paid whether the play is presented for charity or gain and whether or not admission is charged.

Stock royalty quoted upon application to Samuel French, Inc.

For all other rights than those stipulated above, apply to Samuel French, Inc., at 45 W. 25th Street, New York, NY 10010.

Particular emphasis is laid on the question of amateur or professional readings, permission and terms for which must be secured in writing from Samuel French, Inc.

Copying from this book in whole or in part is strictly forbidden by law, and the right of performance is not transferable.

Whenever the play is produced the following notice must appear on all programs, printing and advertising for the play: "Produced by special arrangement with Samuel French, Inc."

Due authorship credit must be given on all programs, printing and advertising for the play.

ISBN 978-0-573-69607-7   Printed in U.S.A.   #29006

No one shall commit or authorize any act or omission by which the copyright of, or the right to copyright, this play may be impaired.

No one shall make any changes in this play for the purpose of production.

Publication of this play does not imply availability for performance. Both amateurs and professionals considering a production are strongly advised in their own interests to apply to Samuel French, Inc., for written permission before starting rehearsals, advertising, or booking a theatre.

No part of this book may be reproduced, stored in a retrieval system, or transmitted in any form, by any means, now known or yet to be invented, including mechanical, electronic, photocopying, recording, videotaping, or otherwise, without the prior written permission of the publisher.

IMPORTANT BILLING AND CREDIT REQUIREMENTS

All producers of *WHO KILLED THE SAUSAGE KING? must* give credit to the Author of the Play in all programs distributed in connection with performances of the Play, and in all instances in which the title of the Play appears for the purposes of advertising, publicizing or otherwise exploiting the Play and/or a production. The name of the Author *must* appear on a separate line on which no other name appears, immediately following the title and *must* appear in size of type not less than fifty percent of the size of the title type.

CHARACTERS

Wilbur Smith
Dolly
Jimmy Smith
Marie Smith
Orville
Cranston Farlow
Sgt. Pete PEterson
Violetta
Sy Goldman

SETTING

The office of sausage king Wilbur Smith.

ACT ONE

Scene One

(The office of sausage king Wilbur Smith. The physical layout of the set is three walls. The fourth wall is open to the audience. There are entrance doors left and right and a door in the rear wall, which leads to the washroom. An ornate desk is angled toward the audience. Behind the desk is a large, executive swivel chair, a throne fit for a "king." The desk contains a computer, phones with intercom capabilities, and various papers and file folders. Two chairs front the desk, and a small couch is along one wall. There are file cabinets, a credenza and other accouterments typical of a working office. There is a large banner on one wall that reads "Get Stuffed with Smith's Savory Sausage.")

(WILBUR SMITH *is at his desk and is shouting into a phone. He is in his shirtsleeves, his tie loosened from an unbuttoned collar. He is comically bellicose, abrasive, and has the demeanor of an uneducated self-made man.)*

WILBUR. *(into phone)* Look...I don't give a damn if he's got Chinese people or not. You tell 'im this is Wilbur Smith, The Sausage King...whadaya mean, am I a friend? Who the hell you think got the crooked bastard elected? If it hadn't been for sausage, he'd still be in the carpet cleaning business...well, you tell Mr. Senator Big Shot as soon as he gets rid of the Chinks to gimmie a call. *(slams receiver)* Loud mouth phony bastard. *(hits the intercom)* Dolly, I need you to take a letter. *(off of the intercom)* Damn politicians, when they're nothing they got their hand out, when they're in office they don't know ya.

(**DOLLY** *enters right carrying a pad and pencil. She slams the door behind her.* **WILBUR** *reacts with a start.*)

Jesus!

(**DOLLY** *is a gorgeous young woman with a body that would stop traffic. Her blouse it tight fitting, revealing her ample breasts, and her skirt is so skimpy that when she crosses her shapely legs her garters and the top of her black hose are revealed.*)

I've told you a thousand times not to slam the door.

DOLLY. Sorry, Willie.

WILBUR. Hey! Never to call me that around the office. You ever call me Willie in front of my wife it'll hit the fan. She's already suspicious enough as it is.

DOLLY. But she's gotta know sooner or later.

WILBUR. Let's make it later.

DOLLY. Why not now? *(sitting, crossing her legs seductively)*

WILBUR. Because I gotta sausage business to think about. And she would get half of everything. She could take over the business. And I gotta obligation to our customers, the sausage eaters of America.

DOLLY. But what about me, Wilbur? I got obligations, too.

WILBUR. What obligations? Manicures, hairdressers, shoes? Hell, I pay you a top salary, pay for your apartment… your garter belts.

DOLLY. But a girl needs security.

WILBUR. What the hell you want me to do, jeopardize everything?

DOLLY. You don't love me.

WILBUR. Don't be silly.

DOLLY. You love sausage more.

WILBUR. Sausage is another matter.

DOLLY. Why not retire? We could move someplace with sun.

WILBUR. And give up the sausage biz? Never.

DOLLY. Your son can take over.

WILBUR. You kidding? The kid's an idiot. He tends to put in too much salt. And we don't see eye to eye. And he's a spendthrift. Buying a Mercedes Benz. Hell, he had the Sausage Mobile.

DOLLY. But I ain't got no future.

WILBUR. Ain't got no future? Jesus, no wonder my letters are the laughing stock of the sausage industry. *(motioning coyly)* Come on over here.

DOLLY. I thought you wanted me to take a letter.

WILBUR. *(lasciviously)* I gotta better idea. Come here.

*(**DOLLY** goes to him and sits on his lap. He runs his hand up and down her leg.)*

Lock the doors.

*(She rises, goes to the doors right and left and locks them. She returns to **WILBUR**.)*

DOLLY. You think this is a good idea?

WILBUR. It beats the hell outta dictation.

(He removes her blouse and pulls off her skirt, revealing sexy under things. He pulls her close and embraces her. Suddenly there is a rattling at the door left. Then pounding.)

DOLLY. Oh, my!

JIMMY. *(off)* Dad! Dad! *(pounding)*

WILBUR. It's Jimmy! Get outta here. Quick

*(**DOLLY** quickly gathers her clothes, runs to the door right and exits, slamming the door behind her causing **WILBUR** to flinch.)*

JIMMY. *(off)* Dad! Dad, you in there?! *(pounding)*

WILBUR. Yes. Yes. I'm Coming! Hold on, for crisesakes!

*(He goes to the door left, unlocks it and opens it, revealing his son, **JIMMY**.)*

What you doing here? Why aren't you in the plant?

JIMMY. I have a problem.

(He enters, slamming the door behind him, causing **WILBUR** *to flinch.* **JIMMY** *is clad in a white smock, a blood-spattered mess due to its exposure to the floor of the sausage factory.)*

WILBUR. Easy with the door, okay? So, what's up?

JIMMY. I can't remember if it's grinding and mixing or mixing and grinding.

WILBUR. What? How the hell can you mix before you grind, gnat brain?

JIMMY. *(He slumps to the couch.)* I keep getting it backwards.

WILBUR. How many times I gotta tell ya? *(enumerating didactically)* It's ingredients, grinding and mixing, stuffing, and thermal processing.

JIMMY. It's hard to concentrate with all of those pigs squealing.

WILBUR. This is the reason, as long as I'm alive, I can't let you take over the operation. God only knows what the customer would get. You think I can turn a going business over to an idiot? What if you mixed up the bologna with the kielbasa? What if you forgot to refrigerate?

JIMMY. *(repeating, counting on his fingers)* Ingredients, grinding and thermal processing, mixing and stuffing.

WILBUR. Christ! What I gotta do, have it tattooed on ya? It's Ingredients, grinding and mixing, stuffing, and thermal processing!

JIMMY. *(Repeating. Leaves the couch.)* Ingredients, grinding and mixing, stuffing, and thermal processing.

WILBUR. And I went and blew good money on a college education. Money down the toilet. I shoulda put you out in the plant after grade school like my dad did me.

JIMMY. *(Repeating. Walking about, trying to remember.)* Ingredients, grinding and mixing, stuff...

WILBUR. *(seating himself behind his desk)* Will you stop it, for God's sake? And sit down, your makin' me nervous.

JIMMY. Okay, okay! I'm just trying to remember.

WILBUR. Remember? Hell, you've been working here for three years.

JIMMY. *(seats himself in one of the chairs fronting the desk)* Don't remind me. Still in the factory, still out there up to my waist in guts eight hours a day, getting ordered around by that bossy Guatemalan woman. I don't know why you don't retire her. She's been here for twenty-five years.

WILBUR. Forget about her. It's none of your business.

JIMMY. You promised to let me take over. But you don't have any confidence in me. If you did, you'd at least put me in charge of stuffing.

WILBUR. And God only knows what we'd wind up with. I can't put that operation in the hands of a college-educated dope. This is a fifty million dollar business here. Smith's Savory Sausage is an international brand. So, relax. You got it made. I'm paying you more than you're worth.

JIMMY. You pay Orville more.

WILBUR. Orville's the plant manager. He's forgot more about sausage that you'll ever know. The man's a worldwide authority on Lebanon bologna.

JIMMY. But I don't have any responsibility.

WILBUR. How can I give responsibility to someone who doesn't know from grinding and mixing?

JIMMY. The illegal immigrants you hire get more respect.

WILBUR. That's because they know what it's like to work for a living.

JIMMY. I'm not cut out to deal with gastrointestinal tracts. It's sickening. If I'd known what I was getting into I would have gotten into something less gruesome – like embalming. I can't take it much longer.

WILBUR. Quit bellyaching. Relax. Wait till I die. Then you can take over the business and run it into the ground without me knowing anything about it. *(shaking and rattling of the door right)* Now what? *(pounding on the door right)*

MARIE. *(off)* Wilbur! Wilbur! Wilbur, are you in there? *(pounding)*

WILBUR. Yes! *(pounding off)* Willya give it a rest, Marie? I'm coming! I've never seen people so damned impatient.

*(He rises and crosses to the door right, unlocks it and opens it revealing his wife **MARIE**. **MARIE** steps into the room, and slams the door behind her. **WILBUR** to reacts with a start. **MARIE** is an attractive woman, noticeably younger than **WILBUR**. She is outrageously overdressed and bejeweled.)*

MARIE. What's with the door being locked?

WILBUR. I was in conference with a person with no memory.

JIMMY. *(standing)* Hi, Mom.

MARIE. Jimmy! Look at you. You look terrible.

JIMMY. What do you expect?

MARIE. Wilbur, how may times have I asked you to give him an office job?

WILBUR. And have him screw up the books?

MARIE. He's out there wallowing in slop day after day, your own flesh and blood.

JIMMY. He treats me worse than the illegal immigrants.

MARIE. *(crosses and sits on the couch)* Well, it has to stop. I won't have it.

WILBUR. *(pacing)* And what happens when he gets authority and our profit goes South? Then what? What happens when you don't have money to blow?

MARIE. What money?

WILBUR. The ten thousand bucks a month I give you, that's what money.

MARIE. Pfft! Nothing.

JIMMY. He's a pinchpenny, Mom. He doesn't give a damn about anything but sausage. Look at me… *(displaying his smock)* his own son, a victim of management suppression.

WILBUR. Yes, and a person with no respect. How you think it made me feel when you stopped driving the sausage mobile?

MARIE. Can you blame him?

JIMMY. It was embarrassing. I couldn't get dates. No self-respecting woman would be seen in the thing.

WILBUR. Nonsense.

MARIE. You can't talk sense to him, Jimmy. He's sausage crazy. "The Sausage King," what a joke.

WILBUR. *(sits behind his desk)* It pays the bills.

MARIE. *(rises, crosses and seats herself in one of the chairs fronting the desk)* On a first date most men show up with flowers or candy, but not your father. Oh, no. He showed up with a box of sausage

WILBUR. You can't blame me for being proud of Smith's Savory Sausage.

JIMMY. You can't reason with him.

MARIE. Why try? It's a waste of time.

JIMMY. Well, I'd better get back to work.

MARIE. Don't lift anything heavy, dear.

JIMMY. *(repeating to himself, enumerating on his fingers as he exits)* Ingredients, grinding and mixing, stuffing, and thermal processing. Ingredients, grinding, mixing, and stuff…*(He exits, slamming door left.)*

DOLLY. A disgrace, that's what it is. You could at least make him plant manager.

WILBUR. And get rid of Orville! Hell, he's the only one around here I can depend on.

MARIE. Offer him early retirement.

WILBUR. The man's a walking meat encyclopedia. He's someone I can talk to. You should hear his recipe for braunschweiger.

MARIE. And you treat him like hell. You have him down there at slave wages.

WILBUR. Where the hell's he gonna go? There ain't a sausage factory on every corner. Besides, I give him a helluva discount on our variety meats. Anyway, what's it to ya?

MARIE. Meat, meat, sausage, sausage. You're obsessed.

WILBUR. Yeah, and my obsession pays for your obsession.

MARIE. How can I be obsessed on ten thousand a month?

WILBUR. Ten grand ain't enough?

MARIE. I'm barely squeaking by. I'm down to my last two bottles of mascara. You're going to have to increase my allowance.

WILBUR. No way!

MARIE. At least double.

WILBUR. What! Hell, woman, are you crazy? I got expenses. Do you realize I have to buy new industrial smokers?

MARIE. I'm not skimping by any longer.

WILBUR. Ten thousand bucks is skimping? Forget it. Not another red cent.

MARIE. Do you realize how embarrassing it is to be seen in the same thing two days in a row?

WILBUR. Then stay home a day.

MARIE. Jimmy's right, you're a cheap, pinchpenny tyrant.

WILBUR. This is what I get for marrying a younger woman. They got no concept of finances. Marie, you're gonna have to squeeze by on ten thousand, because, dammit, this is my limit, this is the...

(The phone intercom buzzes, interrupting him. He goes to his desk and answers.)

Yeah?...What!?...Holy beef jerky!...Okay, I'll be right down. *(slams the receiver)* The Guatemalan woman fell into the grinder. I gotta go.

MARIE. Any excuse to avoid the issue.

WILBUR. *(heading for the door left)* Good God, we may have a woman being turned into sausage down there. And she could be gummin' up a brand new grinder.

*(He exits door left. **MARIE** rises and goes to the washroom door, rear, and enters, slamming the door behind her. **DOLLY** enters right, goes to **WILBUR**'s desk and begins to straighten folders and papers. **JIMMY** enters left.)*

JIMMY. Dolly!

DOLLY. Jimmy! *(They rush to each other and embrace passionately. She pushes him away.)* We have to be careful.

JIMMY. Don't worry. He's got an emergency. *(They embrace again.)*

DOLLY. You think he suspects anything.

JIMMY. Are you kidding? All he thinks about is sausage.

DOLLY. I don't know how much longer I can go on like this. Bouncing back and forth between you and your father.

JIMMY. You think I like it? The thought of his greasy sausage hands all over you makes me crazy. It's driving me nuts. *(losing it)* Nuts!
NUTS!

DOLLY. Easy. Snap out of it!

JIMMY. NUTS!

(She slaps his face quickly, bringing him to his senses.)

Thanks. Sorry. You don't realize what I'm going through day after day, hour after hour.

DOLLY. You think it's easy for me either? But what can I do? Without him I'd be living like a pig.

JIMMY. Please…don't mention pigs.

DOLLY. Your father takes care of me good. With you it's all sex and no future.

JIMMY. Sex is bad?

DOLLY. A girl needs security.

JIMMY. You're too good for him. He's a corrupt businessman who treats people like crap. It's a sad thing to say about your own father, but he's a terrible, unfeeling, stingy person.

DOLLY. I know. He wants to move me into a smaller apartment.

JIMMY. You're better than that. When I take over this business you'll have everything – clothes, diamonds, the best cheap perfume.

DOLLY. But I can't depend on it.

JIMMY. But you're living like a whore.

DOLLY. No situation is perfect. Besides, he's remembered me in his will.

JIMMY. Are you kidding? Hell, he'll never die; he's too full of meat preservatives. And who's to say he won't cut you out?

DOLLY. He'd do that?

JIMMY. As cheap as he is? A man who at Christmas he gives his employees busted cookies?

DOLLY. Maybe something will happen to him before he changes his will.

JIMMY. We can only hope. The world would be a better place without him. Nobody can stand him.

(A toilet flushes, breaking their mood.)

DOLLY. What the…

JIMMY. Someone's in the washroom!

*(They break in panic, **JIMMY** exiting the door left, **DOLLY** the door right, slamming the doors behind them. **MARIE** exits the washroom casually and takes a chair in front of **WILBUR**'s desk. She removes a compact from her purse and checks herself out in its mirror. **WILBUR** enters left, obviously agitated.)*

WILBUR. You still here?

MARIE. I'm not leaving till I get answers.

WILBUR. The answers are all *no!* No, you're not getting more money. No, I'm not buying you a new car. No, I'm not paying for a trip to Europe. Hell, I got real problems to think about here. The Guatemalan woman fell into the grinder. Do you realize the potential for a lawsuit? Thank God she only lost a hand. I had to plead with her not to get a lawyer. And you're bent outta shape because I won't increase your allowance. Jesus!

MARIE. I'm sick and tired of you crying poor.

WILBUR. Someone in this family has to keep his head about finances. I hate to think what would happen if I'd give you or my lame brain son any authority. This place would go down the tubes in six months.

MARIE. My mother warned me about you, she said you'd never support me.

WILBUR. Your mother was a dried up old weasel who drove your father to an early grave.

MARIE. How dare you!

WILBUR. Face it.

MARIE. We had to put him in a home due to early Alzheimer's.

WILBUR. Early Alzheimer's, hell. She drove the poor bastard crazy. He snapped. They picked him up for masturbating in public.

MARIE. That's disgusting.

WILBUR. And so's your spending habits. *(The phone intercom buzzes. He answers.)* She what? Holy Christ! Okay, I'll be right down. *(hangs up the phone)* The crazy broad's making more demands.

MARIE. She's become an embarrassment. Did you see how she was dressed at the Christmas party? Why don't you get rid of her?

WILBUR. You know I can't do that. Now I gotta get back down there and try to reason with her. Hell, if she was still in Guatemala she'd be lucky to be getting a dollar a day for breakin' rocks. *(He heads for the door left.)* And as far as you're concerned, what ever the question is, the answer is no!

(He exits in a huff, slamming the door behind him. ORVILLE enters right, slamming the door.)

MARIE. *(jumping to her feet)* Orville!

ORVILLE. Marie! *(They rush to each other and embrace passionately.)* Darling!

MARIE. Sweetheart!

ORVILLE. What are you doing here?

MARIE. I'm trying to get "The Sausage King" to increase my allowance.

ORVILLE. Good luck. Where is he? We have to be careful.

MARIE. Don't worry. He's down in the plant arguing with the Guatemalan woman about a hand. *(They embrace again.)*

ORVILLE. Do you think he suspects anything?

MARIE. Why would he? He's up to his eyeballs in pork. Obsessed. I don't know how you can work for him.

ORVILLE. It ain't easy.

MARIE. How many years?

ORVILLE. Going on twenty.

MARIE. And he treats you like dirt. It's no wonder you have trouble getting an erection.

ORVILLE. I think it's from over exposure to the saltpeter.

MARIE. As long as Wilbur has control of the purse strings we'll never be together. Even though it's only ten thousand a month, I just can't walk away.

ORVILLE. Maybe he'll have a heart attack.

MARIE. If we're lucky. But the man's strong as an elephant. Maybe somebody in the plant will kill him.

ORVILLE. Everybody down there hates him, even his own son.

MARIE. Can you blame him? A sensitive boy like that being subjected to intestines.

ORVILLE. Marie, we can't keep meeting in cheap motels. I'm starting to smell like disinfectant.

(WILBUR enters suddenly left.)

WILBUR. Orville, why the hell aren't you in the plant?

ORVILLE. I came up to see you about ordering more cloves.

WILBUR. *(crossing to his desk)* After twenty years you can't make a decision?

ORVILLE. But the last time I over-ordered on cloves you took it outta my pay.

WILBUR. *(seating himself behind his desk)* Order five hundred pounds from the lowest bidder. *(turning to* **MARIE***)* And why are *you* still here?

MARIE. I was just leaving when Orville came in.

WILBUR. Well, get the hell outta here. Both of ya. I gotta talk to our lawyers. I got big problems with the Guatemala broad. Hell, you'd think she lost both legs. You'd think living in a country where she gets free medical every time she sneezes would be enough. Okay, outta here!

MARIE. *(She and* **ORVILLE** *head for the door right.)* We'll talk later.

WILBUR. Later is now. Now gimmie some privacy.

*(***MARIE** *and* **ORVILLE** *exit right, slamming the door, causing* **WILBUR** *to flinch.* **WILBUR** *picks up the phone and dials, speaks into the receiver.)*

…Yeah, lemmie talk to Greenbaum…Who? It's Wilbur Smith, The Sausage King…whadaya mean, he's with a client? You tell that overpriced sonofabitch if he doesn't pick up the phone right now he's gonna have one *less* client, okay?…Hello, Sam, I got this woman who fell in the grinder who's making demands…No, it was nothing, only a hand…Right…Well, she's…

(The set suddenly goes black. From the dark, **WILBUR** *lets out a horrendous scream and we can hear the pronounced sounds of a struggle.)*

End of Scene One

Scene Two

*(Lights up on detective **CRANSTON FARLOW**'s office, downstage left. It is a small area consisting of only of a desk with a phone and an ashtray, a swivel chair, and a chair fronting the desk. There is a coat rack with a trench coat, suit coat and hat.)*

*(Super sleuth, **CRANSTON FARLOW**, fastidious in shirt-sleeves, is seated at his desk. **SGT. PETE PETERSON**, a slob in stark contrast to **FARLOW**, is slouching in the chair in front of **FARLOW**, his feet on the desk. He's chewing determinedly on a large, unlit cigar.)*

PETE. So that's the way it is, Farlow. We ain't got nothin', and we been over the scene thirty times. So the chief wants you should come in.

FARLOW. "The Sausage King" case, huh?

PETE. Yeah...the guy who got strangled with a roll of sausage.

FARLOW. He fell victim to his own meat. I've seen his son and widow on the nightly news.

PETE. Wait'll you meet 'em. The son's a goofy little bastard with blood stains all over 'is shirt and the wife looks like Tiffany's window. But not a bad lookin' dame.

FARLOW. Woman.

PETE. The case is draggin' on, and there ain't no evidence and no clues.

FARLOW. But ample motive.

PETE. Right. Cabbage.

FARLOW. Money. They will inherit a fortune. Obviously the greenback has reared its ugly head, has motivated a dreadful act of moral turpitude. So, the police need my assistance, heh?

PETE. I could handle it myself, but the chief was impressed by the way you handled the Myra Finklestein case.

FARLOW. Yes, Peter, but I must confess, I almost missed that one. Finklestein just didn't have the legs of a killer. I could have sworn it was the housekeeper, a mousey little thing with beady eyes and a breath that could beak dinnerware.

PETE. It's usually who ya don't expect. Like in them stories by that English broad. It always turns out to be the guy in the wheelchair who can really walk. Or some old fart that stuffs butterflies. She did have the gams, all right.

FARLOW. Legs. For God's sake, man, gams went out with Alan Ladd. Yes, she had the legs. From the floor up to here…*(hand at his chin)*. Let me ask you, Pete, were those the legs of a murderess?

PETE. Based on legs, no jury would've ever convicted 'er. But you saw past 'em. I gotta hand it to ya, Farlow, you finally cracked the case wide open.

FARLOW. *(correcting him)* Solved the case, Pete. You'd think being a police sergeant for years would have influenced your vernacular. *(recalling)* Yes…it was a matter of deduction, a matter of putting two and two together… the details, the forensics.

PETE. The crime scene gave us nothin'.

FARLOW. Not a clue. It was like the wind had killed her husband.

PETE. Yeah, blown to death.

FARLOW. But she tipped her hand by wearing the sweater with the hollow buttons. When she buttoned up, you could discern that they were hollow.

PETE. What an ear.

FARLOW. That's what alerted me…the perfect place to secrete poison.

PETE. When you put the screws to 'er, she couldn't handle the pressure.

FARLOW. What makes a woman like that tick? She had everything.

PETE. I never seen such ice.

FARLOW. *(correcting)* Jewelry.

PETE. Her old man had to be eighty. He probably couldn't keep up his end of the bargain, if ya know what I mean.

FARLOW. Sexual frustration can be a mitigating factor.

PETE. Yeah, that and fifty million bucks. Plus the mansion, the five cars, and the chauffer with the bulge in 'is uniform. This is the reason I never got married. Too many complications. You get twisted up with dames you never come undone. I gotta hand it to ya, Farlow, fifteen years in this racket and you ain't never blown a case.

FARLOW. *(correcting)* Lost a case. Cranston Farlow, as you so inelegantly put it, doesn't "blow" cases. *(He stands and paces grandly.)* Do you remember the Pangborn case?

PETE. Yeah. Clayton Pangborn, the famous writer.

FARLOW. *(fond reminiscence)* I recall arriving on the scene at three in the morning. It was an inclement night and required me wearing two trench coats. *(expansive, pompous)* It was a bloody mess, I'll tell you…a naked corpse hanging upside down from a chandelier. I was immediately suspicious.

PETE. Yeah.

FARLOW. We cut down the body and laid it on the floor. The forensic people went over the scene with a fine-tooth comb and found nothing. I, however, deduced immediately that it had to be an inside job; someone who knew the chandelier was strong enough to hold a person.

PETE. Maybe the electrician.

FARLOW. That was my first thought before the M.E. arrived, but upon close inspection of the body she found two small puncture holes in its neck.

PETE. Dracula!

FARLOW. Dracula? Nonsense.

PETE. Vampires. I don't give a damn what they say, Farlow, them things exist.

FARLOW. Get a hold on yourself, man. No, it was obviously the work of an insidious fiend, someone who would resort to bizarre tactics to throw the authorities off the scent, and someone who was strong enough to hoist the body. So I turned my attention to the staff. I called them into the study. The housekeeper was a scrawny asthmatic that would have difficulty lifting her feather duster, so she was immediately dismissed. The gardener was an Octogenarian with a clubfoot. The victim's private secretary, however, was a strapping fellow with the temperament of a wolverine, who developed a pronounced twitch under my interrogation. Suspecting a clerical murder, I investigated the victim's desk and found a staple remover with traces of blood. When confronted with this, the man broke down and confessed. Profusely.

PETE. What the hell was the motive?

FARLOW. It came to light that the fellow had been the victim's personal secretary for years and was responsible for correcting his sloppy manuscripts. He'd finally cracked under the pressure of removing faulty syntax.

PETE. A staple remover. I'll be damned.

FARLOW. At trial, I recommended leniency on the grounds of literary insanity. He's currently serving twenty years and is the editor of the prison newsletter.

PETE. It's where the bastard belongs – in the slammer.

FARLOW. *(quickly correcting)* Prison. Well, Peter, my dear unkempt fellow, the case ahead offers challenging obstacles, will require the utmost in investigative diligence.

PETE. *(rising, stubbing out his cigar in the ashtray)* Okay, let's get goin'.

FARLOW. Not so hasty, my impetuous friend. It is necessary that I study in totality all of the facts pertaining to the case and delve into the backgrounds of the suspects. I'll be able to extract cogent information discernable only to the trained observer. We will meet tomorrow.

(The lights fade.)

End of Scene Two

Scene Three

(Wilbur Smith's office. The next morning.)

*(**FARLOW** and **PETE** enter right. **FARLOW** stalks the room, **PETE** sprawls on the couch.)*

PETE. I don't know how anyone can work in this joint. The smell is awful.

FARLOW. *(whipping a ridiculously large magnifying glass from beneath his trench coat)* Only to be obfuscated by the stench of death.

(He moves about the room, observing everything through the heavy lens. He goes to the file cabinet, opens the top drawer and peers into it with his glass.)

Even though the crime scene has been disturbed, there will be clues that are obvious to the trained eye. As it was with the Cyrus Butterball case.

PETE. The turkey magnate who was stuffed to death.

FARLOW. *(prowling the scene)* The authorities had given up all hope until I entered the case. But after through investigation, interrogation, calculation and magnification the pieces fell in to place, revealing the murderer – the ne'er-do-well son in-law. *(entering the washroom briefly, then exiting)* When we shook hands he imparted the distinct odor of thyme, sage, marjoram, rosemary, and black pepper. Pete, I need your assistance. Please take a seat behind the desk.

PETE. Where Old Man Smith was croaked?

FARLOW. Terminated. Yes, I wish to reenact the murder.

*(**PETE** rises and crosses to the executive chair and sits.)*

PETE. *(swiveling)* I ain't never been a vic before

FARLOW. *(standing in the washroom door)* Victim. All right. Considering the room is windowless, there are only three points of entry. From the washroom, the waiting room and the door leading to the plant. I've checked the file cabinet, and, unless the murderer was a midget, we can rule it out as a hiding place. Considering there is no airshaft, we can also eliminate this possibility. Knowing that the lights were doused immediately before the strangulation, the killer had to have come from the washroom.

PETE. How ya figure?

FARLOW. Because it contains the fuse box.

PETE. Brilliant, Farlow.

FARLOW. Merely common sense, my dear ragamuffin. Then the killer rushes behind Smith *(running behind* PETE*)*, applies the sausage in a constricting manner *(He mimes the event.)*, and returns the fuse to the box in the washroom. *(rushes back to the washroom)*

PETE. What happened to the sausage?

FARLOW. *(entering the washroom)* According to the papers, it contained no prints, so it was returned to the widow, who dined on it in a callous act of moral depravity. *(returning from the washroom)*

PETE. The broad ate the murder weapon? What kind of a frail would do a thing like that?

FARLOW. Woman. One possessing an insidious mind capable of any heinous act. These are the kind of people we're dealing with here, Pete. They are crafty, illusive degenerates. But they have never been exposed to the scrupulous methods of Cranston Farlow.

*(*VIOLETTA *enters left. She is a middle-aged woman dressed in peasant garb. Her right arm is heavily bandaged and in a sling.)*

VIOLETTA. Oh! So sorry.

PETE. *(*PETE *leaves the swivel chair.)* Who the hell are you?

FARLOW. Easy, man. *(beckoning)* Come in, my dear, come in.

VIOLETTA. I'm looking for Meester Jimmy.

FARLOW. I'm afraid Mr. Smith is temporarily unavailable.

PETE. Scram. We're on a case here, sweetheart.

VIOLETTA. I come back later.

FARLOW. No, no, it's all right. Are you an employee?

VIOLETTA. Sorry?

PETE. You deaf? An employee? Worker? Do ya work here?

VIOLETTA. Si. I work in grinder part.

FARLOW. *(Stepping forward, extending his hand, which* **VIOLETTA** *takes with her left.)* I'm Cranston Farlow, private investigator, and this is sergeant Peter Peterson. And you are…?

VIOLETTA. My name is Violetta Guadalupe Maria Schwartz.

PETE. Schwartz?

VIOLETTA. Si. My mother marry a Jewish sailor.

FARLOW. I see.

VIOLETTA. Si?

FARLOW. No no, I said, see.

VIOLETTA. Si.

PETE. Hey! Cut the babble, kido.

FARLOW. Have you been employed here for some time?

VIOLETTA. Huh?

FARLOW. Working. Work. *(indicating a chair)* Please, have a seat. Have you been here a long time?

VIOLETTA. *(She sits.)* Si. Twenty-five years. I come to America after leaving Guatemala. Guerrillas come to my village of Jalapa and kidnap the women.

FARLOW. My! What a hideous experience.

VIOLETTA. Si.

FARLOW. Were you familiar with the deceased?

VIOLETTA. Huh?

PETE. *(impatiently waving the unlit cigar in her face)* The guy who was croaked…the dead guy.

FARLOW. Mr. Smith. Did you know him?

VIOLETTA. Oh, yes, Meester Furlong.

FARLOW. *(pompously pacing back an forth in front of her)* Farlow.

VIOLETTA. Si. He was a very good friend. I am very sorry he is dead. He put me in charge of grinder.

FARLOW. Were you on the premises the day Mr. Smith was murdered?

VIOLETTA. Murder!? Oh, my! Yes, I was in the factory looking for my hand.

FARLOW. At what time were you in the factory?

VIOLETTA. Time?

FARLOW. *(pointing to his wristwatch)* Yes. Time. Time. What time *(pointing to the watch)* was it when you were in the plant?

PETE. The time, dumbo!

VIOLETTA. Lunchtime.

PETE. We may as well be talkin' to a rock.

FARLOW. Merely a communications barrier, but I feel the woman may possess cogent information. *(back to* **VIOLETTA***)* What do you know about Mr. James Smith… Jimmy?

VIOLETTA. Meester Jimmy doesn't know stuffing.

FARLOW. I mean, of a personal nature.

VIOLETTA. Personal?

FARLOW. Yes. Personal. You know, special things about him. Secrets.

PETE. This ain't goin' nowhere.

FARLOW. Did Mr. Smith have enemies?

VIOLETTA. Enemas?

FARLOW. No, no – enemies…people who didn't like him.

VIOLETTA. Hum…maybe. I sometime hear him argue with Mrs. Smith and Mecster Jimmy.

FARLOW. Ah ha!

PETE. Now we're gettin' somewhere.

VIOLETTA. And Miss Dolly.

FARLOW. His secretary?

VIOLETTA. Si. Sometimes they make very loud noises. One time I find Miss Dolly and Meester Smith with no clothes on.

FARLOW. Disgusting.

PETE. Damned pervert. This could be a sex caper.

FARLOW. Case. Yes, sex certainly adds to the complexity of the situation. *(He goes to the desk and scans it with his magnifying glass.)*

PETE. What ya doin', Farlow?

FARLOW. *(scanning)* Checking for signs of dalliance.

VIOLETTA. *(rising)* I go back to work.

PETE. *(pushing her into the chair)* Sit down! We ain't through with you, sister.

FARLOW. Easy, man, can't you see the woman's in physical distress?

PETE. I don't think she's comin' clean.

FARLOW. *(returning)* I see no reason to question her further. You may leave, my dear.

VIOLETTA. Thank you, Mr. Fartlow

FARLOW. Farlow.

VIOLETTA. *(rising)* Si.

FARLOW. Pete, although I feel the answer to the riddle lies within a tight circle; I feel it is necessary for us to visit the plant to discern if there was antipathy among the workers. A disgruntled worker may have committed the dastardly deed.

PETE. I already talked to 'em, but they dummied up.

FARLOW. We'll see. *(gesturing to **VIOLETTA**)* After you, Mrs. Schwartz.

*(They exit through the door left. **MARIE** enters right, slamming the door behind her. She goes to the file cabinet, opens the top drawer and removes a manila folder. She ruffles through its contents, finds a document, which she reads with interest. She replaces the document, returns the folder and closes the file cabinet. She exits quickly left, slamming the door. **JIMMY**, **DOLLY** and **ORVILLE** enter right, slamming the door.)*

JIMMY. Where'd he go? We've been sitting out there for over an hour.

ORVILLE. Who is this character, anyhow?

JIMMY. Cranston Farlow.

DOLLY. He's famous. I read all about him.

ORVILLE. Where?

DOLLY. In the bathroom.

ORVILLE. What?

DOLLY. In *Sleuth Magazine*. He cracked the Barrington-Barrington diamond case by finding nose hairs in the jewelry box.

ORVILLE. Well, he gives me the creeps.

JIMMY. He doesn't bother me. *I* have nothing to hide.

ORVILLE. Are you insinuating that *I* do?

JIMMY. You hated Dad for cutting your Christmas bonus.

(**DOLLY** *seats herself in one of the chairs,* **ORVILLE** *sits on the couch,* **JIMMY** *paces.*)

DOLLY. He got a Christmas bonus?

JIMMY. I heard the way you talked about him in the factory.

DOLLY. Yeah!

ORVILLE. Stay outta this, you little tramp.

JIMMY. Watch it, Orville!

ORVILLE. Everybody in the plant knows what's was going on between you two.

JIMMY. If you wanna keep your job around here, you'd better watch it.

ORVILLE. Oh, yeah? And what are you going to do about it? You fire me, who's gonna keep this business afloat? Hell, you don't even know what to do with hog casings. Idiot!

DOLLY. *(stamping her foot)* Quit arguing, it makes my head hurt.

ORVILLE. You have to have a brain to have a headache.

JIMMY. That's it! Clean out your desk.

ORVILLE. I don't have a desk.

JIMMY. Oh, yeah? In that case I'm buying you one.

ORVILLE. But you can't force me to clean it out.

JIMMY. I'm not having you talk like that to the future Ms. Sausage King.

ORVILLE. Oh, so that's it, huh? That's why you killed your father.

DOLLY. You killed your father?

JIMMY. No, no! Of course not. *(pointing to **ORVILLE**)* If anyone around here had a reason to kill him, Orville did. You were jealous of him.

ORVILLE. You had the biggest motive. With your father out of the way you'd never have to drive the sausage mobile again. And you take over the operation.

JIMMY. Watch it, buddy. You were the last one seen with a roll of sausage right before the murder.

DOLLY. Hey, you're right. Right before the lights went out I saw him with it.

ORVILLE. That's a lie. And what about you, little Miss Sausage Heiress? I saw you reaching for something under you skirt.

DOLLY. I was adjusting my garter belt.

ORVILLE. You had as big a motive as anyone.

JIMMY. That's ridiculous. Dolly wouldn't hurt a fly.

DOLLY. Of course not.

JIMMY. She's a good person with bad shorthand. So don't go pointing fingers. What about you and that woman in animal carcasses? You were seen several times carrying on with her behind a dead steer.

ORVILLE. *(jumping up from the couch)* Look, I don't have to take this from a stupid upstart like you.

JIMMY. Oh, Yeah!?

ORVILLE. Yeah!

DOLLY. *(standing, holding her head)* Stop it! Stop it, you two!

JIMMY. Okay, okay.

ORVILLE. She's right, what the hell are we doing? We have to stick together.

JIMMY. Yeah, you're right. Especially with this crazy detective snooping around.

MARIE. *(entering right)* Oh, there you are. *(She slams the door behind her.)*

JIMMY. Mom! Where've you been?

MARIE. In the factory. I saw that numbnuts policeman and that detective snooping around down there. He was looking at loaf of headcheese through his magnifying glass.

JIMMY. We were just discussing how we have to keep our cool.

ORVILLE. We don't wanna make him suspicious.

MARIE. He looks like a crafty one.

DOLLY. He solved the Pinkton Rathbone case.

JIMMY. Where?

DOLLY. In *Sleuth Magazine*. He figured out that nobody had killed him, that Rathbone had choked to death on his own dandruff.

FARLOW. *(Entering left, followed by* **PETE** *and* **VIOLETTA**.*)* Ah, ha! The flock has gathered.

JIMMY. Or course. What do you expect?

ORVILLE. You think we're gonna sit out there all day cooling our heels?

FARLOW. I apologize for the inordinate delay.

ORVILLE. Well, I'm outta here. I gotta sausage factory to run.

MARIE. And I have and appointment with my spiritual advisor.

JIMMY. And I'm not hanging around here all day. No way.

PETE. Can the excuses, okay? You're gonna stay here till we get this thing ironed out.

DOLLY. So, you're Cranston Farlow.

FARLOW. Yes, one and the same.

DOLLY. Wow! Can I have your autograph?

FARLOW. Why, of course.

DOLLY. *(taking a paper and pen from the desk)* I been reading all about you; about the Barrington-Barrington and Pinkton Rathbone cases. Gee.

(Returning to **FARLOW** *with the pen and paper.* **FARLOW** *signs the paper with a flourish.)*

I've never met anyone smart before.

PETE. Hey! Cut the chatter, baby. Can't you see we gotta murder to solve here?

FARLOW. Easy, Peter…all in good time. The young lady is obviously a devotee of the criminal arts.

DOLLY. I am?

FARLOW. Now, as to the matter at hand…I'm afraid it will be necessary to speak with each of you individually.

DOLLY. *(flirty)* Can I be first?

JIMMY. This'll take all day.

MARIE. Outrageous!

ORVILLE. Do you realize we have sausage overheating down there?

PETE. Zipper yer traps, all of ya? Would you like that I take the bunch of ya downtown?

FARLOW. That won't be necessary, Pete. In fact, it is Important that I conduct my inquires at the scene of the crime. Now, if you don't mind, we will…

(The lights suddenly go to black. There are screams and disruptive sounds.)

End of Scene Three

Scene Four

(The group is in the same position as before, with the exception of **VIOLETTA** *who is lying on the floor with a piece of beef on her face. The players, with the exception of* **FARLOW** *and* **PETE**, *react with expressions of horror.)*

JIMMY. Holy crap!

MARIE. Oh, my God!

ORVILLE. Jesus!

PETE. *(clearing them from the body)* Stand back! Everyone!

FARLOW. And don't touch anything.

PETE. Not even yourselves.

MARIE. This is terrible.

DOLLY. *(trembling)* This ain't in my job description.

ORVILLE. Another murder.

JIMMY. And it's not even noon.

FARLOW. *(kneeling next to* **VIOLETTA***)* Insidious. *(lifting the slice of beef from her face)* Suffocated. Murder by beef.

MARIE. *(looking away)* Awful.

FARLOW. *(handing the beef to* **PETE***)* Here.

(Pete takes the meat and places it on the desk. **FARLOW** *whips out his magnifying glass and examines the body closely.)*

This is even more malign than the Milton Henshaw case, where the victim was volumed to death by electronic music.

DOLLY. The poor woman.

JIMMY. How do we know she's poor? She could have millions stashed away in Guatemala City. She coulda killed Wilbur.

ORVILLE. Why would she want to commit murder? She wasn't even union.

FARLOW. *(rising)* She obviously knew the identity of Smith's killer.

PETE. Yeah. And that person's gotta be in this room.

JIMMY. What!

MARIE. No!

DOLLY. Well, it ain't me. I'm a vegetarian.

FARLOW. Yes…I'm afraid the murderer is among us.

ORVILLE. That's ridiculous.

FARLOW. And each of you has easy access to beef.

PETE. The joint's crawlin' with it.

MARIE. This is an insulting accusation.

PETE. Stifle the whining

FARLOW. *(moving to the head of the body)* Here, Pete, give me a hand with the body. We'll remove it to the waiting room. *(placing his hands under* **VIOLETTA***'s armpits)* Take hold of her feet.

PETE. *(taking* **VIOLETTA***'s feet)* Don't none of ya leave the room. Understand? We got questions to ask ya.

(He and **FARLOW** *lift the body and move with it toward the door right.)*

JIMMY. Why would any of us want to kill a sausage grinder?

FARLOW. *(moving toward the door)* Someone in this room had motive.

ORVILLE. This is insane.

MARIE. Outrageous.

DOLLY. Until she lost a hand, I never heard of 'er.

*(**FARLOW** and **PETE** exit right with the body.)*

JIMMY. *(to* **ORVILLE***)* You worked right next to her.

ORVILLE. So, what?

JIMMY. So, she probably had something on you.

ORVILLE. What about you? You resented her because she knew more about the sausage business.

DOLLY. Jimmy wouldn't do such a thing.

ORVILLE. You're a great one to talk. I wouldn't put anything past you, you ignorant little gold-digging bimbo.

JIMMY. Watch it! Don't you dare talk like that to my future wife.

MARIE. Future wife!

DOLLY. Jimmy and me are gonna get married.

MARIE. Over my dead body!

ORVILLE. Not a good choice of words.

MARIE. I'm not having this pea-brain get her hands on my son's money.

JIMMY. You can't stop us.

MARIE. She killed your father.

JIMMY. What!?

DOLLY. I didn't kill no one.

MARIE. She had a motive. The idiot left her in his will. I saw the papers.

ORVILLE. *(pointing to* **DOLLY***'s attire)* A woman who dresses like that is capable of anything.

JIMMY. You stay out of this, bologna brain. You had more incentive than anyone. You hated him for not promoting you to the head office. And you probably killed the Guatemalan woman because she knew you killed Dad.

ORVILLE. Watch it, buddy! What about you? You hated your old man because he wouldn't turn the business over to a numbnuts.

DOLLY. *(holding her head)* I think I'm gonna be sick.

MARIE. You're going to be sicker when you find yourself behind bars.

DOLLY. That's silly, I don't even drink. And look who's pointing fingers. You killed poor Wilbur because he wouldn't give you a bigger allowance. I heard you one day when I was in the washroom adjusting my unmentionables.

JIMMY. Is that right, Mother?

MARIE. Don't listen to her, she's sailing without a boat.

DOLLY. Oh yeah!?

MARIE. Yeah!

(She lunges at **DOLLY** *who recoils and races away,* **MARIE** *in hot pursuit.* **MARIE** *chases* **DOLLY** *round and round the desk.)*

I'll teach you to accuse me, midget mind!

DOLLY. Get her away from me! She's crazy!

JIMMY. Mom! Stop it!

MARIE. *(chasing)* Just wait'll I get my hands on the murdering little bitch!

DOLLY. *(fleeing)* Help!

JIMMY. That's enough!

DOLLY. She's the killer. Look at her beady eyes. She's crazy!

MARIE. *(lunging at **DOLLY**)* I'll show you crazy!

JIMMY. Mom! For God's sake!

*(He lunges at **MARIE** and subdues her.)*

What's the matter with you?

MARIE. *(struggling)* Let me go!

JIMMY. Don't you realize how this would look to that phony gumshoe? We gotta stick together.

ORVILLE. He's right, Marie.

MARIE. *(struggling)* Nobody's going to accuse me of murder. Especially some little streetwalker.

JIMMY. *(restraining **MARIE**)* Well, you'd better get used to her, because she's gonna be your daughter-in-law. Besides, she hasn't been a streetwalker for years. So, settle down, okay?

MARIE. Well...

ORVILLE. At a time like this, we can't afford to be at each other's throats.

MARIE. *(stops struggling)* All right, all right, okay. I just hope you don't plan to have children with this person and further the white trash population.

DOLLY. See...she's mean and crazy.

JIMMY. *(releasing **MARIE**)* Okay, that's enough! Both of you. Now look, all of you, we have to get our stories straight here. We didn't see anything we didn't hear anything. Okay?

DOLLY. I'll dummy up.

MARIE. That shouldn't be hard.

FARLOW. *(entering right, followed by **PETE**)* We'll leave her out there for the M.E. Now, where were we?

PETE. You were gettin' ready to grill the creeps.

FARLOW. Interrogate the suspects.

DOLLY. I ain't a suspect, I'm a secretary.

PETE. Clamp yer trap, kid.

FARLOW. It is patently obvious that one of you murdered the poor, unfortunate creature and also killed "The Sausage King."

PETE. It's an open and shut case, and inside job, as plain as the nose on your face, a slam dunk, a…

ORVILLE. *(holding his ears)* Oh, no! Stop it! I can't take it!

PETE. What the hell's the matter with you…you nuts?

ORVILLE. No, I'm allergic to idioms.

PETE. What the hell you talkin' about?

FARLOW. Enough of this. Let's get down to brass tacks.

ORVILLE. God…he's doing it, too.

PETE. Hey! Cut the crap, all of ya. I had my way you'd all be downtown.

MARIE. You have nothing to hold us on.

JIMMY. Why would any of us wanna kill the woman?

FARLOW. Perhaps one of you had a moral antipathy toward Guatemalans.

PETE. Yeah, and one of ya coulda hated foreigners.

MARIE. That's nonsense.

DOLLY. I didn't know 'er well enough to hate 'er.

FARLOW. Enough of this. It's time for one-on-one probing.

DOLLY. *(touching her hair seductively)* Why, Mr. Farlow…

PETE. He means talkin' to ya one at a time, airhead.

FARLOW. I'd like to begin with Mr. James Smith. So, if the rest of you will be good enough to leave the room, I'll…

(The set suddenly goes black. Shouts of frustration and general panic: "Good God! Jesus! What the hell? My pants! My skirt! Good heavens!" etc. Extended sounds of pandemonium. Lights up revealing the cast in states of undress; **DOLLY** *and* **MARIE** *in sexy underwear,* **JIMMY**, *and* **ORVILLE** *are without pants.* **FARLOW** *and* **PETE**

are the only members clothed as before. The group stares at each other with expressions of disbelief and embarrassment. Then they react to a stranger in their presence. He is wearing a white laboratory coat, and large horn-rimmed glasses; his long, unruly hair is protruding from beneath a large floppy hat. He's carrying a clipboard and ballpoint pen.)

ORVILLE. Where'd you come from?

PETE. Yeah. Who the hell are you?

SY. I'm Sy Goldman, the sausage inspector.

End of Act One

ACT TWO

Scene One

(Immediately following. The group is still stunned by the entrance of sausage inspector, **SY GOLDMAN**.*)*

PETE. Now look here, Glodstone...

SY. Goldman.

PETE. You can't come bustin' in here like this; we're in the middle of a murder investigation.

JIMMY. Yeah. And what happened to our regular inspector?

SY. He got trichinosis due to over-exposure to pork.

FARLOW. I'm afraid, Mr. Goldman, that this isn't an opportune time.

SY. I'm authorized by the state to carry out periodic inspections and this is the day.

FARLOW. In that case, you may proceed.

JIMMY. We were just inspected two weeks ago.

SY. That may be, but I still have to have a look at your factory. We've had a bunch of complaints.

ORVILLE. Who from?

SY. That's confidential.

FARLOW. Obviously from a disgruntled employee. Perhaps the person responsible for these heinous acts.

SY. *(consulting his clipboard)* There's a long list of violations. *(He enumerates.)* Improper disposal of animal carcasses, poor lean-to-fat ratios, meat contaminated with bacteria and other microorganisms, over-seasoning, employees not washing their hands for at least twenty minutes before handling meat products. The list goes on.

JIMMY. I always wash my hands.

DOLLY. If you don't believe it, look at his fingernails.

ORVILLE. This is ridiculous. I wanna know who stole my pants.

DOLLY. Yeah. And my dress.

MARIE. What dress? You may as well have been wearing a Kleenex.

SY. This is another violation. You can't be running abound half-naked around sausage. *(noting on his pad)* I'm writing you up for semi-nudity in the presence of meat.

PETE. Okay, Goldbloom...

SY. Goldman.

PETE. Whatever. Take your clipboard and clear the hell outta here. We gotta get on with our investigation.

FARLOW. Yes. I suggest you conduct your inspection within the confines of the plant.

SY. Who was murdered?

PETE. None of your damned business.

FARLOW. Wilbur Smith, "The Sausage King." Were you acquainted?

SY. No. But I've read about him in *Sausage Business*. A helluva guy. He knew more about curing jerky than anyone. The man was a pioneer. He's in the Sausage Makers' Hall of Fame. He was a winner of the Golden Wiener.

MARIE. What does all this have to do with anything?

JIMMY. A waist of time.

MARIE. Standing around talking about Wilbur's wiener while I'm freezing my buns off.

ORVILLE. *(heading for the exit left)* I'm looking for my pants.

PETE. Hey! *(blocking his path)* You're not goin' anywhere, pal.

FARLOW. Yes. Nobody leaves this room without my permission, because one of you is not only a crafty assassin, but also a deft practitioner of swift clothing removal. Now...it's necessary that I interrogate you individually.

Starting with Mr. James Smith. Pete will accompany the rest of you to the plant.

DOLLY. Why can't we wait in the outer office?

FARLOW. Because I don't want you to contaminate the body of the unfortunate Guatemalan.

SY. *(pointing to the door right)* That was a dead body? I thought the woman was asleep. *(noting on his pad)* I'm writing you up for a 602.

JIMMY. What the hell's a 602?

SY. *(writing)* Dead people within a hundred feet of emulsified products.

ORVILLE. For Christ's sake, Goldblatt.

SY. Goldman.

PETE. All right, all right! That's enough! All of ya outta here except Smith. Follow me. And no funny stuff.

FARLOW. Thank you, Peter.

(**PETE** *exits left followed by everyone but* **JIMMY**.)

Have a seat, James.

(**JIMMY** *sits.*)

All right, let's revisit the day of your father's untimely demise.

JIMMY. Couldn't we look for my pants first?

FARLOW. All in good time. *(paces dramatically)* Your pants are no doubt a critical part of the equation and must be considered relative to the successful conclusion of this case. But the pants, excuse the expression, will have to take back seat.

JIMMY. You don't actually think I killed my father?

FARLOW. You had ample motive. And working in a slaughterhouse day after day could have inured you to the brutality of death.

JIMMY. I hate it. When they kill the pigs, I hide in the men's room.

FARLOW. But why weren't you repulsed enough to quit?

JIMMY. Because…if I quit I'd have to look for work.

FARLOW. A feeble excuse.

JIMMY. I'm no good at job hunting. I tried it and nobody would hire me.

FARLOW. Where were you at the time of the murder?

JIMMY. Having a peanut butter and jelly sandwich at the Elite Café. I eat there everyday.

FARLOW. *(quickly in **JIMMY**'s face)* Chunky or plain!?

JIMMY. Chunky. I like the crunch.

FARLOW. I've always preferred the texture of plain. What time did you leave the plant?

JIMMY. Exactly at noon.

FARLOW. Do you have any witnesses?

JIMMY. The waitress at the Elite.

FARLOW. I'm going to need her name.

JIMMY. Her name is Zina. She's a big woman with a Hungarian accent and a large mole on her nose.

FARLOW. *(quickly in **JIMMY**'s face)* Which side!?

JIMMY. I don't remember.

FARLOW. You eat there every day and can't remember? Highly unlikely.

JIMMY. *(squirming)* I'm not good at details. Like stuffing and grinding. I also misplace my car keys a lot.

FARLOW. The report states that you discovered your father.

JIMMY. Right after lunch. He was *(pointing)* slumped in that chair with a roll of sausage around his neck.

FARLOW. What did you do?

JIMMY. I called to police.

FARLOW. You sure you made the call?

JIMMY. Yes.

FARLOW. The police report that they were unable to identify you as the caller.

JIMMY. That's because I had peanut butter in my teeth.

FARLOW. *(in **JIMMY**'s face)* Don't lie to me, young man. You returned from lunch, killed your father and phoned the authorities in a disguised voice in a callous act of self-centered depravity.

JIMMY. No! Why would I wanna do that?

FARLOW. Why? I'll tell you why. Because you're the heir to a sausage fortune. When you found him, in which position was the body?

JIMMY. Upright.

FARLOW. Earlier you said slumped.

JIMMY. He was slumped in an upright position.

FARLOW. He couldn't be slumped and upright simultaneously.

JIMMY. Come to think of it, maybe he was more like leaning.

FARLOW. *(quickly in **JIMMY**'s face)* To the right or left!?

JIMMY. *(confused)* Or maybe he was slumped upright in a leaning position. I'm not sure.

FARLOW. A convenient lapse of memory. He was either slumped or upright or leaning, and if he was leaning it stands to reason it had to be either left or right. Which is it?

JIMMY. I think he was leaning left in a slumped, upright position.

FARLOW. Don't play with me, young man. And your waffling won't play with a jury. *(He whips his magnifying glass from his trench coat and studies **JIMMY**'s face at close proximity.)*

JIMMY. *(recoiling)* What are you doing?

FARLOW. I'm looking for signs of guilt-induced stress. Constricted lines about the eyes are very revealing. *(peering at **JIMMY**)* Why did you kill your father?

JIMMY. *(jumping up)* Get that thing out of my face! I can't take it!

FARLOW. *(replacing the magnifying glass)* You packed your lunch, consisting of a peanut butter and jelly sandwich, which you consumed in the plant, faked leaving the premises, returned to this office with a roll of sausage and strangled your father.

JIMMY. *(wringing his hands)* That's not true! I couldn't hurt anyone. I'm even nice to insurance salesmen.

FARLOW. That's your story. The records, however, show that you often argued with your father regarding your salary and that you were a disgruntled employee.

JIMMY. You have no idea what he was like. His whole life was sausage. From the time I was baby it was sausage, sausage, sausage. Morning, noon and night. At bedtime he'd read me sausage recipes. I'd have nightmares about how organ meats and even blood could be made delicious by grinding and spicing. Instead of *Goodnight Moon*, every night he read me *The Little Sausage that Could*.

FARLOW. This is no excuse for an act of cool-blooded murder.

JIMMY. *(pacing, wringing his hands)* Anybody could have killed him; everyone hated him.

FARLOW. There are also rumors of dalliance between you and your father's secretary.

JIMMY. Dolly and I are very much in love.

FARLOW. Ah ha! Now it comes out.

JIMMY. Who could resist her? You saw her garter belt.

FARLOW. And she was, no doubt, a willing accomplice in your heartless scheme to eliminate you father.

JIMMY. Dolly couldn't hurt anyone. She's a wonderful girl. Generous. She gives ten percent of her salary to Porn Stars Anonymous.

FARLOW. And she was no doubt using you to get to your father's money. She prodded you, withheld sexual favors. It's a common scenario. Lady Macbeth.

JIMMY. Who?

FARLOW. Lady Macbeth.

JIMMY. Was she in the sausage business?

FARLOW. Of course not. See here, my friend, it won't serve you well to play dumb with me. You may present a façade of childish innocence, but your nervous behavior indicates otherwise. You had every motive to commit sausageside.

JIMMY. *(falling into a chair, head in hands)* You're wrong. I didn't do anything.

FARLOW. Then, during the confusion, while the lights were out, you smothered the poor, handless Guatemalan with a cut of raw beef.

JIMMY. Why would I wanna do that?

FARLOW. Because she undoubtedly possessed information linking you to the crime.

JIMMY. I hardly knew the woman.

FARLOW. After working with to her for years?

JIMMY. She was weird. She was too Guatemalan. And she was crazy. She used to talk to the meat.

FARLOW. *(standing over **JIMMY**)* Your excuses are a thin veneer covering the heart of a serial killer.

JIMMY. Serial? Only two people are dead.

FARLOW. That we know of. Where have you buried the others?

JIMMY. Huh?

FARLOW. Don't dummy up.

JIMMY. I don't know what you're talking about.

FARLOW. That's because you're in denial. You're not only a pathological liar; you're also a cruel perpetrator of multiple murders. Studies have proven that overconsumption of peanut butter leads to psychopathic behavior. As in the case of Harlan Millbank, the Chicago murderer who went on a killing rampage after eating two jars of Skippy.

JIMMY. I wanna talk to a lawyer.

FARLOW. Ah ha! This proves you're insane. No one in his right mind wants to talk to a lawyer.

*(The left door flies open and **DOLLY** rushes in followed by **MARIE** and **PETE**.)*

PETE. *(chasing)* Stop it, you two!

MARIE. Just wait till I get my hands on you, you little bitch.

DOLLY. Help! *(They race around the desk.)* Keep her away from me! She's crazy!

MARIE. *(pursuing)* Come back here you cheap little slut!
JIMMY. *(jumping up)* Mom! Stop it!
PETE. *(chasing)* Stop, dammit! Come back here, you two!

(They make another lap around the desk and exit through the right door.)

FARLOW. Stay out of there, you'll contaminate the Guatemalan!

(There is noise, shouting and confusion offstage, then they re-enter, race across the set and exit left, slamming the door behind them. More shouting offstage. FARLOW *and* JIMMY *stand in stunned silence.* PETE *re-enters left, slamming the door behind him.)*

PETE. *(out of breath, slumping to the couch)* Let 'em kill each other. I ain't in any kinda shape for this anymore. Farlow?

FARLOW. Yes?

PETE. The Guatemalan broad. She's gone.

FARLOW. Gone? What do you mean gone?

PETE. Gone. She ain't in the waiting room.

FARLOW. That can't be. *(heading for the stage-right door)* Impossible. *(Exits right. Returns quickly, slamming the door.)* She's gone!

PETE. That's what I said.

JIMMY. How can dead people be gone?

FARLOW. Something's afoot.

PETE. No kidding.

FARLOW. The case is deepening in complexity.

JIMMY. *(trembling)* I hate dead people. They make me nervous. And it's even scarier when dead people disappear.

PETE. Shut up!

FARLOW. Let's not be harsh.

PETE. We're gettin' nowhere, Farlow. I say we take 'em all downtown, put 'em under the lights an' break out the rubber hoses.

FARLOW. Calm yourself, for heaven's sake. We're not resorting to cruel, archaic, inhuman tactics. Pete, take this serial killer to the plant and bring back the young woman.

JIMMY. Dolly? She didn't kill anyone. And I'm not a serial killer.

FARLOW. That remains to be determined.

PETE. *(grabbing* **JIMMY** *by the collar and dragging him left)* C'mon, mouse-mind.

(Exits with **JIMMY** *stage left, slamming the door.* **FARLOW** *whips the magnifying glass from his trench coat and inspects the area.* **PETE** *enters left with* **DOLLY** *in tow.)*

PETE. Here she is.

FARLOW. *(indicating a chair)* Sit down, my dear.

(She sits.)

PETE. You want I should slap her around?

FARLOW. Or course not.

PETE. But I haven't slapped anyone around lately. I don't wanna lose my touch. *(nostalgic)* I haven't slapped anyone around since I was a guard in cell-block 16 at Hartsdale prison. Them were the days. How 'bout I just cuff her a little bit around the ears?

FARLOW. Nonsense. This case will be solved by intellect.

PETE. *(heading for the door left)* Okay, have it your way, but I say we work 'er over.

(He exits stage left. **FARLOW** *circles* **DOLLY**, *observing her through his magnifying glass.)*

FARLOW. *(studying)* Hum. Yes. Interesting. Yes, very interesting indeed.

DOLLY. What 'cha doin'?

FARLOW. Let me ask you. Were you ever dropped on your head as a baby?

DOLLY. I can't think that far back.

FARLOW. Try.

DOLLY. Well…the first thing I remember was my Uncle Fred overhauling the clutch on his Ford pickup.

FARLOW. Did you know that you have a misshaped cranium?

DOLLY. No. Wow! Is it catching?

FARLOW. Of course not. What ever gave you that idea?

DOLLY. Well…my cousin, Clark, he had a lopsided head. He had a problem keeping a hat on.

FARLOW. Ah ha! A congenital connection. *(returning his magnifying glass to his trench coat)* Damage to the head at an early age often leads to criminal behavior.

DOLLY. So far as I know Clark was a model prisoner.

FARLOW. You're cousin was incarcerated?

DOLLY. No. He had all of his foreskin.

FARLOW. What!?

DOLLY. Ain't this conversation gettin' kinda personal?

FARLOW. In a criminal investigation we have to probe the suspects.

DOLLY. *(touching her hair coquettishly)* Probing? Why, Mr. Farlow.

FARLOW. No no! You don't understand.

DOLLY. No need to be shy.

FARLOW. My intensions are purely professional.

DOLLY. I ain't born yesterday. I've had men approach me before. Of course they weren't as famous as the person who solved the Barington-Barington murder.

FARLOW. Now look here, miss…

DOLLY. Dolly. As long as you're gonna to probe me I think we oughtta call ourselves by our first names.

FARLOW. Will you please stop it!?

DOLLY. You started it. I'm just an innocent person tryin' to cooperate with the police.

FARLOW. I'm not the police. I'm a private detective.

DOLLY. A dick?

FARLOW. I beg your pardon? No…a private investigator.

DOLLY. That's good. This way it'll be private. Between you and me. And you can count on me not to tell a soul.

FARLOW. *(growing frustration)* There isn't going to be anything to tell.

DOLLY. Of course not, because it'll be private. Lemme ask you, did you probe anyone during the Barrington-Barrington case?

FARLOW. Of course. Many people.

DOLLY. Oh, dear. You're a devil, ain't you?

FARLOW. Enough of this! *(quickly)* Where were you at twelve noon on Wednesday, April 12?

DOLLY. How would I know?

FARLOW. Because it was the time of the murder.

DOLLY. I can't remember.

FARLOW. *(dramatically pompous)* I'll tell you where you were. Let me refresh your memory. You were sequestered in the washroom with Mr. James Smith. Smith had faked going to the Elite café and returned to this office where he jointed you in the washroom with a roll of sausage. When Smith removed a fuse from the box, you grabbed the sausage, ran from the washroom and strangled Wilbur Smith in an act of gross indifference. Don't deny it.

DOLLY. I never touched any sausage.

FARLOW. *(circling **DOLLY**)* You had every motive. It has come to light that "The Sausage King" remembered you in his will. Also, Wilbur Smith's death would result in his son, Jimmy, taking over the business, a happenstance that would result in you benefiting as James's wife. You both planned the murder in meticulous detail and executed it flawlessly. You had no compunction to being a confederate in this crime as well as an accomplice in serial killings. *(quickly in her face)* Where did you bury the bodies!?

DOLLY. I don't know what the hell you're talkin' about. How could I have been in the washroom with Jimmy when I can't remember where I was?

FARLOW. What!

DOLLY. I think you're confused.

FARLOW. *Me* confused? How dare you!

DOLLY. And I thought you were smart. If I you was you wouldn't go around probing people. What if I decided to tell *Sleuth Magazine*?

FARLOW. Tell them what?

DOLLY. About all the people you probed during the Barrington-Barrington case. How you accused me of bein' in the washroom when I don't remember where I was? How would it look, Mr. Big Shot Probing Detective?

FARLOW. Apparently you aren't grasping the gravity of the situation.

DOLLY. *(jumping up)* I ain't grasping anything, just like I didn't grasp any sausage. *(heading for the door left)* You gotta lot of nerve. Wanting to probe a poor innocent girl like myself.

FARLOW. Stop! Come back here!

(She slams out of the stage left door. **PETE** *enters right, slamming the door behind him.)*

PETE. I can't figure out where the Guatemalan broad's body got to. I've looked all over the damned place.

FARLOW. Obviously removed by the killer to deflect my investigation.

PETE. What's with the Dolly dame?

FARLOW. She is wholly uncooperative, displays skewed logic and has an accusatory nature.

PETE. And a body on her that won't quit. You can't trust a dame with a build like that.

*(***MARIE** *and* **ORVILLE** *enter left.)*

What the hell are you two doin' up here?

MARIE. We're not spending any more time around that Goldfarb character.

FARLOW. Goldman.

ORVILLE. He's driving everyone nuts. Running around with his clipboard, nosing into everything. He's giving everyone warnings. He even wrote up a pig for loitering.

MARIE. The man's crazy.

ORVILLE. Some people don't know how to handle authority.

PETE. So what? Stifle the bitchin' and wait'll we call ya.

FARLOW. No no, it's all right, Pete. I was going to interrogate them next.

PETE. You want I should stick around?

FARLOW. No, thank you. Please be good enough to continue your search for Mrs. Schwartz.

PETE. You think maybe someone dumped her in the grinder? If so, she could show up in stores all over America.

MARIE. Ew. What a thought.

FARLOW. It's a distinct possibility. The mind we're dealing with here is capable of the most hideous atrocities.

PETE. Okay. If ya need me, I'll be checkin' the grinder for jewelry. *(He exits left.)*

FARLOW. *(indicating the chairs fronting the desk)* Please be seated.

*(**MARIE** and **ORVILLE** seat themselves, and **FARLOW** seats himself in the "Sausage King's" chair. He swivels about, tapping his chin thoughtfully.)*

All right, imagine that I'm Wilbur Smith.

MARIE. But you don't look a thing like him.

FARLOW. Of course not. That's not the point.

ORVILLE. What *is* the point?

FARLOW. The point is, I'm replicating the presence of the victim to determine the psychological impact upon your consciences in order to establish the whole from the sum of the parts.

MARIE. I don't get it.

FARLOW. It's called Gestalt. All right, imagine me with a roll of sausage constricting my neck.

*(He leans back in the chair. Silence. He slumps forward, elbows on the desk, glaring intently at **MARIE** and **ORVILLE**.)*

Just as I thought. Guilty! You both stiffened at the sight, a positive sign that it reminded you of the dastardly crime you committed.

MARIE. We didn't kill anyone.

FARLOW. So it's "we" is it?

MARIE. I meant "I."

FARLOW. But you said "we." It's a Freudian slip.

MARIE. *(looking down, fingering her underwear)* No, it isn't… it's Victoria's Secret.

FARLOW. It's obvious you conspired to eliminate Wilbur Smith.

ORVILLE. Look…even though we had our disagreements, I wouldn't kill him.

FARLOW. You both had motive. I've studied this case. You think I'm a naïf with respect to its particulars? And since Mr. Smith's untimely demise you have been seen about town in open displays of intimacy.

MARIE. We're just good friends.

FARLOW. Good "friends" don't check into the Heavenly Mattress Motel without luggage.

MARIE. We were visiting someone from out of town.

FARLOW. Till nine o'clock the next morning? Come come. The affair between you and Orville here is well documented. And you will inherit a sizable estate. And you, sir, will be elevated within the organization to executive status. What do you have to say to this?

MARIE. I say I'm innocent.

FARLOW. Even though the Guatemalan women often heard you in heated discussions with the deceased?

ORVILLE. She was lying.

MARIE. You'd take the word of a one-handed peasant over that of a grieving widow?

ORVILLE. The woman was a phony. Her green card was chartreuse. And she claimed to be half Jewish but she couldn't have been because she handled pork.

FARLOW. Where were you at noon on Wednesday, April 12?

ORVILLE. In the plant, rendering fat.

MARIE. I was getting a manicure.

FARLOW. I'm going to need that manicurist's name.

MARIE. It's Rochelle, but she's blind. She won't know if I was there.

FARLOW. *(rising from behind the desk, pacing dramatically)* You're both lying. The case is coming into focus. Both being possessed of hatred and avarice, you carefully planned the murder of Wilbur Smith "The Sausage King." While you were conversing with your husband, Orville sneaked into the washroom where he lurked with the murder weapon – six feet of unseasoned sausage. I say unseasoned because no residue of salt our other preservatives were found on the victim's neck. After Orville here plunged the office into darkness, you entered and shoved a half-eaten peanut and jelly sandwich into your husband's mouth to quell his screams. Orville left the washroom and applied the stricture the ended your husband's life. Orville returned the fuse and you both left the scene with cold-blooded nonchalance. *(suddenly spins in their direction at close proximity)* Don't deny it!

MARIE. We didn't do anything.

FARLOW. *(pointing at the desk)* Then how do you explain traces of peanut butter on this desktop?

ORVILLE. We don't like peanut butter.

FARLOW. Ah ha! So it's "we" again, is it? You work in concert in carrying out your crimes.

MARIE. Crimes?

FARLOW. There have been a rash of Murders in this vicinity all with traces of peanut butter left at the scenes.

ORVILLE. You're crazy! *(**FARLOW** whips the magnifying glass from his trench coat and begins to scrutinize **ORVILLE**'s face.)*

ORVILLE. Get that thing outta my face!

FARLOW. Guilt's written all over it.

MARIE. *(peering at **ORVILLE**)* I don't see anything written on him. Although he does have the word "Mother" tattooed on his left forearm.

FARLOW. I'm not surprised. The criminal element often defaces the body. *(putting the glass away)*

ORVILLE. We're innocent, I'm telling you.

FARLOW. Of course. So were Leopold and Loeb.

MARIE. Who?

ORVILLE. Leopold and Loeb. They played for the Giants.

FARLOW. No, I'm afraid they were cold-blooded murderers just like the two of you.

MARIE. Look...my husband may have been a tight-fisted philanderer who treated people like dirt, but nobody's perfect. And even though I couldn't stand him, I wouldn't kill him. And Orville couldn't kill anyone.

ORVILLE. And Marie's a kind-hearted person who wouldn't hurt a soul.

MARIE. Thank you, dear.

FARLOW. Don't attempt to cover for each other. It won't wash. You come across as devious confederates.

(PETE enters from left, slamming the door.)

FARLOW. Yes, Peter?

PETE. It's that Goldblatt character. He's driving everybody nuts. Sorry, didn't mean to interrupt ya, Farlow.

FARLOW. That's perfectly all right, my friend, I was just concluding my interrogation.

PETE. You outta let me deal with these slimy weasels.

FARLOW. Suspects.

PETE. I still say a little pain goes a long way.

FARLOW. Not true. Besides, due to employing the deductive process, meticulous observation and precise cross-examination, I have arrived at conclusions that have resulted in my reaching positive conclusions.

PETE. Huh?

FARLOW. Please be good enough to summon James and the tempestuous young woman.

MARIE. I won't be in the same room with her.

FARLOW. I'm afraid that's unavoidable.

PETE. *(exiting left)* I'll be right back. *(exits, slamming the door)*

ORVILLE. *(noting his wristwatch)* You got any idea what time it is?

FARLOW. Yes. It's time for the pigeons to come home to roost, to pay the piper, to face the consequences, to face the music, to own up, for the fat lady to sing, for the...

ORVILLE. *(holding his head)* Stop it! I can't stand it!

MARIE. Orville! Get hold of yourself!

ORVILLE. The idioms again. I can't take it!

FARLOW. These uncontrollable outbursts triggered by figurative language are indicative of a deep-seated pathology. I strongly advise psychological evaluation.

MARIE. He never behaves this way with his pants on.

*(**PETE** enters left followed by **JIMMY** and **DOLLY**.)*

PETE. Here they are, Farlow.

FARLOW. Very good. Now...please make yourselves comfortable.

*(**DOLLY** seats herself on the small couch and **JIMMY** stands near her. **MARIE** and **ORVILLE** remain in their chairs. **PETE** stands to one side. **FARLOW** walks about dramatically, and then seats himself behind the desk where he taps his fingertips together thoughtfully. There is a pregnant silence. He clears his throat.)*

As is obvious, each of you had strong motives to kill "The Sausage King," motives driven by issues of the flesh coupled with an insatiable desire for gain – a volatile combination. Never, since my involvement with the Cuthbert Willingham case, have I encountered such lust and avarice. This case, however, while on the surface open and shut, is one of subtle complexities. *(He stands and crosses to **MARIE**.)* You, my dear, clearly would financially benefit from the demise of your husband. With him out of the way you would inherit handsomely and could openly pursue you romantic involvement with Orville. You also carried great animus toward Wilbur due to him limiting your allowance.

MARIE. You don't realize. I couldn't even buy decent cosmetics.

FARLOW. Be that as it may, you had strong motives for murder. *(above* **ORVILLE***)* And you, my dear sir, also stood to gain greatly. A loyal, underpaid, under appreciated employee, an acclaimed authority on sausage who played second banana, was seething with hatred that had simmered for years. Also, as lover and, no doubt, potentially the future husband of Mrs. Smith, you stood to financially benefit while rising within the company.

ORVILLE. But I wouldn't kill him. I'm not a murderer!

FARLOW. So you say, so you say. But realities would have one believe otherwise. *(moving to* **DOLLY***)* And here we have a woman whose apparent ignorance belies the fact that she is a calculating jezebel with a lopsided head that was carrying on clandestinely with both father and son, playing both ends against the middle.

DOLLY. I was never in the middle. Whadaya you take me for?

FARLOW. For a conniving woman who realized that with Wilbur Smith out of the picture she would become the wealthy wife of James Smith.

DOLLY. You wouldn't dare talk to me this was if I had my clothes on.

FARLOW. You had every incentive to strangle Wilbur Smith

JIMMY. She couldn't hurt anyone.

FARLOW. So she would have you believe. *(moving to* **JIMMY***)* You were easily duped because your emotions had conquered your reason. And what about you, Mr. James Smith?

JIMMY. What about me?

FARLOW. You had every reason to want you father dead. This way you would inherit the business, become "Sausage King Junior" and be free to marry a floozy. You hated your father for forcing you to drive the Sausage Mobile, work in the plant, and for calling to attention your gross ineptness in front of your fellow employees. You wanted him dead.

JIMMY. But I could have waited. His cholesterol was 360.

FARLOW. But waiting would not have been expedient. Under pressure from you paramour, you could not wait to carry out your dastardly plan.

JIMMY. No! I didn't kill "The Sausage King!"

ORVILLE. None of us did.

DOLLY. Except maybe his wife.

MARIE. Why, you little bitch! *(rising threateningly, moving toward* **MARIE***)*

DOLLY. Keep her away from me!

PETE. *(placing himself between* **DOLLY** *and* **MARIE***)* That's it! Cut the crap! Both of ya. *(***MARIE** *sits.)*

FARLOW. I have painstakingly analyzed the minute details of this case and have…

(He is interrupted by the entrance of **SY GOLDMAN** *left.)*

PETE. What the hell?

SY. I've finished my inspection.

PETE. Then get the hell outta here!

SY. *(noting his clipboard)* You got numerous violations. *(enumerating)* Refrigeration is often above forty degrees, pathogenic bacteria is possible due to slow cooling, a high possibility of bacterial contamination and food borne illness due to…

PETE. That's enough! Mail 'em a copy.

SY. I'm also writing you up for an 814.

JIMMY. What the hell's an 814?

SY. Not reading animals their rights before slaughtering.

ORVILLE. That's ridiculous.

SY. It's the law. Pigs vs. California 618.

PETE. Farlow, you want I should throw this nut case out?

FARLOW. No, quite the contrary. It's important he remain for my summation.

SY. I outta be going. I gotta file my report.

PETE. You heard what the man said. You ain't goin' nowhere.

*(***SY** *moves in the direction of the washroom.)*

Hey! Where you think you're goin'?

SY. To the washroom.
PETE. Freeze creep!
FARLOW. It's all right, Pete. We must never deny the exigencies of the bladder.

*(**SY** enters the washroom.)*

Now, as I was saying, I have painstakingly analyzed the minute details, scrupulously checked backgrounds, and assiduously scoured the police files with respect to all of the suspects in this case, and have determined the identity of the killer. *(moving about the room and stopping before* **JIMMY***)* Even though my suspicions were aroused early on, I felt it necessary to question each of you as a failsafe against rash judgment. You, James, even though you had every motive to kill your father, could never have committed such an act. Your benign temperament and repulsion to the horrors of the plant expose a person of a kind, sensitive disposition. *(moving to* **DOLLY***)* And you, my dear, even though your misshapen head and rustic insensibilities would lead one to believe you are capable of murder, I sense in you a person of childish naiveté who was compromised by a unenviable situation. Also your answers and attitude, while ludicrous, were genuine in nature. *(moving to* **MARIE***)* As for Mrs. Wilbur Smith, your self-centeredness and narcissism would prevent you from committing an act that would place you in prison and outside the advantages of cosmetic alteration and beautifying accouterments. *(moving to* **ORVILLE***)* And lastly, our good friend Orville. You sir, even though you were sublimated to the roll of an underling and daily humiliation and are illicitly involved with Mrs. Smith, you had much too much respect for the expertise of "The Sausage King" to perpetrate his murder. Even though a ruthless, tight-fisted and insensitive manager, he imparted to you knowledge, which makes you a living authority on the fine art of sausage making. Now…I hasten to apologize to all of you for putting you through the rigors of intense interrogation. Even though I was nearly certain of the killer from the beginning, it was necessary to eliminate all suspects in order to justify my suspicions.

PETE. Okay then, Farlow, who the hell it?

MARIE. Yes. Who is it?

JIMMY. I told you I didn't do it.

DOLLY. Don't keep everyone in suspense like you did in the Barrington-Barrington murders.

PETE. Yeah. Come on, Farlow.

FARLOW. Please, calm yourselves. All right…the murderer is…

(The set is plunged into darkness. There are screams, shouts and general confusion. Lights up. **FARLOW** *emerges from the washroom dragging* **SY GOLDMAN** *by the scruff of the neck.)*

Here, ladies and gentlemen, is your murderer!

ORVILLE. What?

MARIE. The sausage inspector?

PETE. Goldstein?

FARLOW. Goldman. *(dragging* **SY** *to the vacant chair and slamming him into it)* But, in fact, his name isn't Goldman. In fact, he is not a he…*(He rips the hat and a wig from* **SY**'s *head exposing* **VIOLETTA.***)* "He" is Viloetta Guadalupe Maria Schwartz!

JIMMY. What the…?

PETE. The Guatemalan broad?

DOLLY. But she's dead.

FARLOW. *(holding* **VIOLETTA** *in the chair)* So she would have us believe.

MARIE. I don't understand. I thought she was a victim of meaticide.

FARLOW. Nothing more than a crafty, ingenious ruse.

MARIE. But why would she want to kill Wilbur?

ORVILLE. And how could she strangle him with one hand?

FARLOW. She never lost a hand. She faked it being severed as a means of diverting suspicion. This is what first peaked my interest. When I first met her her arm was bandaged. The bandage, however, showed no seepage of blood. A result of a severed hand would be profuse bleeding. She also showed no signs of agony to an injury that would have been excruciating.

JIMMY. But why would she wanna kill my father?

FARLOW. Because she's your mother.

JIMMY. What!?

MARIE. What are you talking about?

FARLOW. Violetta Guadalupe Maria Schwartz is Jimmy's real mother.

MARIE. This is crazy! I'm his mother!

FARLOW. So you would have everyone believe. But, after diligent research, while delving into the background of each suspect, I discovered that twenty-five years ago, you and Wilbur adopted a baby boy from Guatemala, and that this was simultaneous with the hiring of Mrs. Schwartz as sausage grinder at this facility. No mere coincidence.

PETE. I'll be damned.

JIMMY. Jesus! I'm not who I think I am!

MARIE. Don't listen to him, Jimmy. The man's a pompous liar.

FARLOW. You may cast aspersions Madame, but the records indicate otherwise. And you and Mr. Smith covered up Violetta's identity because she blackmailed him by threatening to go to the media with the story of your husband's dalliance while in Guatemala, a liaison that resulted in Jimmy's birth.

JIMMY. I don't believe it.

FARLOW. Why do you think Mrs. Schwartz has been employed here for twenty-five years at a salary of a hundred thousand a year?

ORVILLE. A hundred thousand?

DOLLY. That's crazy. I see her paychecks.

FARLOW. *(moving among them)* The hundred thousand is off the books. Do you realize that Mrs. Schwartz resides at 2004 Country Club Drive in a home of architectural significance? She has parlayed her earnings into a sizable estate. Mrs. Smith, you have been complicit in this cover up for years because you realized that the truth would result in the downfall of this business. How would it have looked to the sausage consumer if it had been revealed that Wilbur Smith impregnated an innocent peasant in the Guatemalan jungle and had been concealing his love child? Disaster.

ORVILLE. But if Wilbur was her meal ticket, why would she wanna kill 'im?

FARLOW. *(pacing, smug in his knowledge)* Because she could no longer control her festering resentment. Even though she was enjoying the fruits of her wrongdoing, she had been seething with hatred for a quarter century. And she had hatched a perfect plan; strangling Wilbur Smith with his own sausage, thus diverting suspicion to those who would stand to benefit from his demise. Then she went to the diabolical extreme of faking her own death as a means of eliminating herself as a suspect. Then, with bold self-confidence, she returned, disguised as a sausage inspector, and deftly removed your clothing in order to confuse you and set you at each other's throats. Damned clever. But her disguise failed to mask traces of Yiddish-Guatemalan in *(Making parentheses signs with his fingers.)* "Goldman's" speech, nuances my trained ear detected immediately. Also...*(Plunging his hand into a pocket of* **VIOLETTA***'s lab coat, withdrawing a small, rectangular object and holding it aloft dramatically.)*

ORVILLE. What's that?

FARLOW. An electronic device by which she controlled the lighting. Ingenious.

JIMMY. I still can't believe it. My own mother's not my own mother.

MARIE I would have told you, Jimmy, but there was too much jewelry at stake.

DOLLY. You mom's a murderer. This means bad blood. Our kids could grow up to be the Manson Gang.

JIMMY. *(stamping his foot)* I don't wanna be Jewish.

FARLOW. Relax, young man, you should be proud of your Jewish heritage. And remember, you are also part Guatemalan-a gentle and noble race.

JIMMY. Alluva sudden, *(snapping his fingers)* just like that, I'm a Guatemalan Jew. Damn.

PETE. Quit the beefin'. In fact all of ya got no complaints. You should all be grateful that Farlow figured out the real killer. Now you can get on with your twisted, perverted lives. And I don't want any trouble from any of ya in the future. Not even a parkin' ticket. Understand?! *(hovering over* **VIOLETTA***)* And you...you rotten, murderin' bitch, you're goin' down. Do you get what I'm sayin', sister?

VIOLETTA. Si.

PETE. Well...whadaya got to say for yourself?

VIOLETTA. *(with a shrug)* Oi vai.

(Curtain)

Also by
Roger Karshner...

Clothes Encounters
Don't Say Goodbye, I'm Not Leaving
The Dream Crust
Hot Turkey at Midnight
Love on the Cusp
The Man with the Plastic Sandwich
Monkey's Uncle
To Live at the Pitch
Where There's a Will There's a Relative

Please visit our website **samuelfrench.com** for complete descriptions and licensing information

OTHER TITLES AVAILABLE FROM SAMUEL FRENCH

DEAD CITY
Sheila Callaghan

Full Length / Comic Drama / 3m, 4f / Unit Set
It's June 16, 2004. Samantha Blossom, a chipper woman in her 40s, wakes up one June morning in her Upper East Side apartment to find her life being narrated over the airwaves of public radio. She discovers in the mail an envelope addressed to her husband from his lover, which spins her raw and untethered into an odyssey through the city... a day full of chance encounters, coincidences, a quick love affair, and a fixation on the mysterious Jewel Jupiter. Jewel, the young but damaged poet genius, eventually takes a shine to Samantha and brings her on a midnight tour of the meat-packing district which changes Samantha's life forever—or doesn't. This 90 minute comic drama is a modernized, gender-reversed, relocated, hyper-theatrical riff on the novel Ulysses, occurring exactly 100 years to the day after Joyce's jaunt through Dublin.

"Wonderful... Sheila Callaghan's pleasingly witty and theatrical new drama that is a love letter to New York masquerading as hate mail... [Callaghan] writes with a world-weary tone and has a poet's gift for economical description.
The entire dead city comes alive..."
- *New York Times*

"*Dead City*, Sheila Callaghan's riff on James Joyce's Ulysses is stylish, lyrical, fascinating, occasionally irritating, and eminently worthwhile... the kind of work that is thoroughly invigorating."
- *Backstage*

SAMUELFRENCH.COM

OTHER TITLES AVAILABLE FROM SAMUEL FRENCH

JACK GOES BOATING
Bob Glaudini

Full Length / Comedy / 2m, 2f / Interior
Four flawed but likeable lower-middle-class New Yorkers interact in a touching and warmhearted play about learning how to stay afloat in the deep water of day-to-day living. Laced with cooking classes, swimming lessons and a smorgasbord of illegal drugs, *Jack Goes Boating* is a story of date panic, marital meltdown, betrayal, and the prevailing grace of the human spirit.

"An immensely likable play [that] exudes a wry compassion."
- *The New York Times*

"Endearing romantic comedy about a married couple and the social-misfit friends they fix up. Witty and knowing and all heart."
- *Variety*

"Glides effortlessly from the shallow end of the emotional pool to the deep end."
- *Theatremania.com*

SAMUELFRENCH.COM

www.ingramcontent.com/pod-product-compliance
Lightning Source LLC
Chambersburg PA
CBHW070650300426
44111CB00013B/2353